Pasta & Potatoes
An Irish~Italian Girl Cooks

Kelly Schweiger

Copyright © 2014 Kelly Schweiger

All rights reserved.

ISBN: 1477486445
ISBN-13: 9781477486443

DEDICATION

This book is dedicated to my family, both immediate and extended – past, present and future. The roots from which our family tree has grown and thrived, are so important to us here in the present and will continue to make us strong for the generations to come.

And….as always, I dedicate this book to my husband and my children.

ACKNOWLEDGMENTS

I would like to thank my wonderful sister-in-law, Kim, for her unending patience, her time, her know how, and her honesty. She was a wonderful editor and sounding board. I hope she knows just how much her help with this book, which is so close to my heart, truly means to me.

CONTENTS

Chapter 1 : The Basics _____ 7

Chapter 2 : Soups & Starters _____ 21

Chapter 3 : Breads _____ 36

Chapter 4 : Sides _____ 46

Chapter 5 : Entree _____ 53

Chapter 6 : Desserts and Treats _____ 70

Index _____ 87

About the Author _____ 89

I decided to write this book because I believe that food is a language of love that a family uses to speak to one another. It transcends time and flows from one generation to the next. Families use familiar foods to knit together their celebrations and their sorrows, and to speak to one another. Think about it…think of how you show someone you care - when someone is sick, has a baby, a birthday, a housewarming, or even a death, food can be your words when you think you have no words.

Food provides an anchor for our memories and a focal point for family gatherings. All families have recipes that have become the bright and colorful threads weaving their way through each generation. Every new twist on a recipe, because of marriages, travel, emigration, etc., adds to the old pattern and is passed down to the newest generation.

The recipes in this book represent the many threads that make up my history. Irish and Italian mostly, some very old, some with a new twist – these are the things , the threads, that I want to pass down to the next generation so that they can add to our rich family tapestry in their own way. My husband shares a similar heritage, so I have included some recipes from his family as well. This crazy and amazing tapestry of food did not start with me, and I encourage you all to add to your own family's quilt in your own individual ways.

Chapter 1 : The Basics

Everyone has to start somewhere right?

This chapter includes what I would consider some 'basics' that will make your cooking experience that much better. These are simple things that will enhance not only the recipes in this book but your cooking and baking in general. Included here are also a few simple recipes and techniques that will be used in other recipes throughout this book and some 'base' recipes that you can play with to make your own.

Roasting Garlic

Garlic. It is an amazing thing. Garlic is often associated with Italian cooking, and rightly so. However, garlic (or garleog) is also very important to the people of Ireland. Garlic's flavor sweetens and mellows when it is roasted. It adds a wonderful depth of flavor to recipes but is equally delicious on its own. Don't be scared! The flavor is nothing like raw garlic. When it is roasted it is mild and almost nutty.

A few of my Italian ancestors

- Whole heads of Garlic (any kind)
- Olive oil

Take the head (leaving it whole and the skin on) turn it on its side and cut the top off of the head, about ½ inch down. Basically, you want to expose the garlic enough so that it's easy to get out once it's roasted. Set the garlic in your baking dish. Generously drizzle with olive oil. Pour it on so that the oil seeps in all over. Repeat with as many heads as you want to make. Now, you can either wrap each head tightly in foil or if you are doing a lot and would like to save the infused oil…just cover the baking pan tightly with foil. Roast in a 350 degree preheated oven for 30- 45 minutes. Garlic is done when it is lightly browned and soft all the way through. Squeeze the head to pop out the soft-yummy-wonderful cloves. Leftovers can be stored in the freezer to use at a later date.

Clarified Butter (ghee)

Clarified butter (also called drawn butter or ghee) is used in places where you'll be frying something either for an extended period or over high heat and for those times when you want the flavor of butter, rather than oil.

Clarifying butter removes the milk solids and moisture. Keep in mind when you clarify you'll lose about 25% of the volume of butter. Clarified butter will keep for 3 to 6 months in the refrigerator.

- Unsalted Butter

Heat the unsalted butter in a heavy-duty saucepan over very low heat, until it's melted. Let simmer gently until the foam rises to the top of the melted butter. When it looks like no more foam seems to be rising to the surface, remove from heat and skim off the foam with a spoon. (this buttery foam can be used on warm bread or over steamed veggies or the like) Then slowly pour the butter through a strainer with a few layers of cheesecloth. That's it! You now have clarified butter.

***TIP: If you continue to heat the butter after it melts without removing the solids, it will slowly begin to turn a light nutty brown. This 'browned butter' is very tasty and is called for in many recipes. Just be careful not to burn it!

Roasted Red Pepper

- Fresh Red Sweet Peppers

Start by washing the peppers well.. Now they need to be charred on high heat by roasting them in the oven (which is what I like to do) or on a grill. Use tongs to turn the pepper to blacken on all sides.

If roasting in the oven, preheat to 450°F. Arrange the peppers on a foil covered cookie sheet and roast in the oven, turning every 15 minutes until blackened on all sides (about 30 minutes).

Once they are done, place in a covered bowl or brown paper bag. The steam from the peppers will make the skin easy to slide/peel off. Once the peppers have cooled, carefully peel (with your fingers or a knife) the blackened skin and discard. Pull or cut off the top of the pepper and squeeze gently to remove the seeds.

Never rinse or wash the peppers or you will lose that wonderful smoky flavor. When the skins and seeds have been removed, cover the peppers in olive oil, and refrigerate for up to two weeks.

Basic Chicken Stock

Chicken stock is easy to make and it freezes well. You can freeze it in plastic freezer bags, your favorite plastic container, or freeze it in an ice cube tray (than pop out the 'cubes' and throw them in a freezer bag. These small servings are great for when you only need a little bit of stock for a sauce)

You can make beef, chicken, vegetable or fish stock. The process for all is pretty much the same - add everything to a big pot, add water, simmer, simmer, simmer….then strain and eat or freeze.

I will give you a good base for a chicken stock. You can add or change up the ingredients to suit what you have and what you like.

***TIP: This same recipe can be used for beef, veal, fish or even vegetable stocks. Instead of chicken bones just add the beef or veal bones, lean fish bones/heads…or no bones at all in the case of vegetable stock!

<u>Chicken Stock</u>
- chicken legs, thighs, backs, bones, and/or wings (about 5-6 pounds)
- 3 large onions paper skin peeled off and quartered
- 6 large carrots peeled cut in half
- 8 stalks celery with leaves cut in half
- 5 sprig fresh thyme
- 2 bay leaves
- 1 whole clove garlic - peeled
- 8 peppercorns
- 16 cups water

Place chicken, vegetables, and herbs and spices in a huge stockpot. Add water and cook on high heat until you begin to see bubbles break through the surface of the liquid. Turn heat down to medium low so that stock maintains low, gentle simmer. After a little while you will see a "scum" form on the top of the water. Skim this scum from the stock with a spoon or mesh strainer several times during the first hour of cooking and then as needed. Add hot water as needed to keep bones and vegetables submerged. Simmer uncovered for 6 to 8 hours.

Strain stock through a fine mesh strainer or cheese cloth into another large stockpot or heatproof container discarding the solids. Cool immediately to below 40 degrees. Place in refrigerator overnight. Remove solid fat from surface of liquid in the morning and store in container with lid in refrigerator for 2 to 3 days or in the freezer.

My Great-Great Grand Father on
the Irish side of the family!

Basic White Sauce (Béchamel)

- 2 tablespoons butter (oil or other fats can also be used)
- 2 tablespoons flour
- 1 cup cold milk (or cream)

In a small, heavy saucepan, melt 2 tablespoons of butter over low heat.. Blend 2 tablespoons of flour into the melted butter. This is called a roux.

Add 1/4 teaspoon of salt. Cook over low heat, stirring, for 4 to 5 minutes. This will minimize the 'flour' taste. Now whisk in COLD milk. The trick to a smooth white sauce is HOT roux and COLD milk.

Whisk well over medium heat until thickened. The sauce can be made thicker or thinner by increasing or decreasing the amount of roux used.

***TIP : You can use a roux and instead of milk use broth or pan drippings to make a tasty gravy or soup base.

Basic Pizza Dough

Pizza dough is great...you can make pizza of course but you can also make so many other things...it is a very versatile dough. Calzones, pretzels, garlic knots, stromboli, focaccia bread, bread sticks, etc...play around and see how many uses you can come up with.

- 2 packets (¼ ounce each) active dry yeast
- 2 tablespoons sugar
- ¼ cup olive oil, plus more for bowl and brushing
- 2 teaspoons coarse salt
- 4 cups all-purpose flour - plus more for work surface
- 1 ½ cups warm water

Pour water into a large bowl; sprinkle with yeast and let stand until foamy, about 5 minutes.

Whisk sugar, oil, and salt into yeast mixture. Add flour and stir until a sticky dough forms. Transfer dough to an oiled bowl and brush top with oil. Cover bowl with plastic wrap and set aside in a warm, draft-free place until dough has doubled in bulk, about 1 hour. Turn out onto a lightly floured work surface and gently knead a few times before using.

The dough can be frozen in a plastic freezer bag for up to 3 months.

Basic Tomato Sauce

This is the most basic form of tomato sauce. Throughout this book you will find other sauces (or gravy if you are Italian). But if you just want a quick simple tomato sauce this is all you need.

- 1 (28 ounces) can chopped tomatoes
- 1 (28 ounces) can crushed tomatoes
- 3 cloves garlic, pressed and minced
- 1 small onion diced small
- ¼ cup extra-virgin olive oil
- 1 teaspoon sugar
- ¼ teaspoon salt
- 2 teaspoons dried oregano and basil

In a 3-quart saucepan, heat the olive oil over medium heat. Add the onion and garlic, and cook until soft, about 8 to 10 minutes. Add tomatoes with their juices to the pan. Add sugar and bring to a boil. Lower heat and simmer 15 minutes add seasoning and herbs. Simmer another 10 minutes

***TIP: Sauce can be made ahead of time and kept covered in the refrigerator for up to 3 days or frozen for up to 3 months

My Grandfather, Mom, Aunt, and Grandmother

Basic Pasta Dough

This is the most basic pasta dough recipe there is. It contains only 3 ingredients that everyone has in their house. You can have homemade pasta anytime! There are other pasta recipes in this book but this is a great place to start.

- 2 cups unbleached flour
- 3 eggs
- Pinch of salt (optional)

On a clean dry work surface, make a mound of the flour and, using your fingers, make a well in the center of the mound. Crack the eggs one by one and drop the eggs into the center of the well you made of the flour. With a fork, beat the eggs together. Again using the fork, slowly begin to fold the flour in towards the center of the well to incorporate the flour into the beaten eggs. A doughy mass will eventually begin to form. Work this mass using your fingers until it begins to feel uniformly dry. Then begin to knead the dough with both hands. To knead; use the palms of both hands, pushing from the center of the ball of dough outwards and folding the near edge inwards to begin the kneading cycle again, making a quarter turn with the dough each time. The kneading stage should take about 10 minutes by hand.

After the dough has been fully kneaded, it is time to thin the dough into sheets suitable for cutting. A manual pasta machine works wonders at this stage. Cut the ball of dough into three equal pieces. Form these pieces, by hand, into equal rectangular shape to be passed through the rollers of the pasta machine. Set the cylindrical rollers at their widest opening, put a piece of dough in the space between rollers and crank the handle to pass the dough through. As the sheet of pasta comes out the bottom of the rollers it should be set on a floured cotton towel to rest while you begin on the next piece. Repeat the thinning process with the remaining pieces of pasta, thinning and then setting aside, so that each piece of pasta is equally rolled out. When all the pasta has passed through the first rolling stage, set the machine to the next setting to begin rolling the pasta thinner. Start the rolling process again, beginning with the first piece of dough and continue with the remaining pieces. As each is rolled thinner set it aside and continue onto the next. This process can be done with a rolling pin as well, just be sure to roll in one direction and flour your pin. Either way the dough should be very thin.

When they are all rolled out you are ready to cut the pasta into the desired shape. They can be cut using the cutting wheels of the rolling machine or by hand using a knife.

Fresh pasta cooks extremely fast…especially if you make it and use it immediately. Literally a minute or two depending on how thick it is will be all you need. Pasta can be dried.

Caramelized Onions

- 2 or 3 large onions sliced
- 2 tablespoons oil
- 2 tablespoons brown sugar

In a skillet over medium heat, in hot oil, cook until tender. Stir in sugar and cook until golden.

Italian Vinaigrette

- ½ cup good olive oil
- ½ cup red wine vinegar
- 1 tablespoon Dijon mustard
- 1 scallion minced
- ¼ teaspoon oregano
- ¼ teaspoon thyme
- 2 fresh basil leaves torn up small
- 1/8 tea cracked black pepper
- 2 tablespoons lemon juice

Combine all and whisk well…or shake in a jar

***TIP: Always save the rind when you buy parmesan cheese. Wrap it and throw it in the freezer...it adds TONS of flavor to soups and stews and other recipes

Basic Pesto

- $2/3$ cup pine nuts, toasted lightly
- 6 cups loosely packed fresh basil leaves
- 3 garlic cloves, chopped
- sea salt and freshly ground pepper
- ½ cup extra virgin olive oil
- 1 cup grated Parmesan cheese

Blanch the basil very briefly (to preserve its color and flavor.) To Blanch: First prepare an ice-bath in a large mixing bowl. Bring about a quart of water to boil, add about a tablespoon of salt. It should taste like sea water. Submerge the basil leaves for a second or two at most and then immediately remove and plunge into the ice bath. Pat leaves dry.

In a food processor or blender, combine toasted nuts, basil leaves and garlic until well-combined. While machine is running, pour in olive oil in a slow, steady stream, until smooth. Season with salt and pepper.

Stir in grated cheese just before serving.

Basic Risotto

- 1½ cups arborio rice
- 1 qt chicken stock
- ½ cup white wine (optional)
- 1 medium shallot or ½ small onion, chopped (about ½ cup)
- 3 tablespoons unsalted butter
- 1 tablespoon vegetable oil
- ¼ cup grated Parmesan cheese
- 1 tablespoon chopped Italian parsley or basil
- kosher salt, to taste

Heat the stock to a simmer in a medium saucepan, lower heat and keep stock hot but not boiling.

In a large, heavy-bottomed saucepan, heat the oil and 1 tablespoon of the butter over medium heat. When the butter has melted, add the chopped shallot or onion. Sauté for 2-3 minutes or until it is slightly translucent.

Add the rice to the pot and stir it briskly with a wooden spoon so that the grains are coated with the oil and melted butter. Cook for another minute or so but don't let the rice turn brown.

Add the wine and cook while stirring, until the liquid is fully absorbed.

Add a 1 cup of hot chicken stock to the rice and stir until the liquid is fully absorbed. When the rice appears almost dry, add another cup of stock and repeat the process until all stock is absorbed.

It's important to stir constantly, especially while the hot stock gets absorbed, to prevent scorching, and add the next cup of stock as soon as the rice is almost dry.

 Continue adding stock, a cup at a time, for 20-30 minutes or until the grains are tender but still firm to the bite, without being crunchy. If you run out of stock and the risotto still isn't done, you can finish the cooking using hot water. Just add hot water as you did with the stock, a ladle at a time, stirring while it's absorbed.

Stir in the remaining 2 tablespoons butter, the parmesan cheese and the parsley/basil, and season to taste with Kosher salt.

Risotto turns glutinous if held for too long, you should serve it right away. A properly cooked risotto should form a soft, creamy mound on a dinner plate. It shouldn't run across the plate, nor should it be stiff or gluey.

My Grandfather, Grandmother Doria Costantini Bernitt, my Mom, Aunt and a friend.

Chapter 2 : Soups & Starters

Traditionally the first course is designed to stimulate the desire to eat. Whether served as a part of the meal or as an appetizer the effect is the same… However, sometimes you just want a small meal and any of the recipes in this chapter would work as a light meal or snack.

Kelly's Cock-a Leekie Soup

- 8 cups of water
- 1 stewing chicken (3-4 pounds) giblets removed
- 4 - 6 large leeks washed and sliced discarding the tough upper green leaves
- 1 bay leaf
- 1 stalk lemon grass (cut away lower bulb and tough outer leaves retaining the yellow main stalk)
- ¾ cup pearled barley
- ¼ cup fresh parsley chopped (or you can use baby spinach or kale chopped)
- ½ teaspoon salt
- ½ teaspoon cracked black pepper

In a large 6 qt soup pot add water, chicken, ½ the leeks, bay leaf, salt and pepper. Prepare your lemon grass by cutting the yellow stalk into 2-3 inch lengths. Then "bruise" these sections by bending them several times. Make superficial cuts along these sections with a knife, which will help release the lemon flavor. Add these bruised stalks to the pot. Bring to a boil over high heat. Skim off foam . Reduce heat and simmer covered. Skim as needed. Simmer for 2 hours or until chicken falls away from the bone.

Carefully using a slotted spoon transfer chicken to a plate and cool. When it is cool remove skin and pick meat from the bones and return the meat to the pot. Add the barley and the rest of the leeks to the pot and return to a boil. Reduce heat, simmer covered for 20 minutes or until barley is tender. Remove bay leaf and lemon grass. Stir in parsley and serve.

Potato Leek Soup

- 4 -5 medium leeks
- 3 tablespoons butter
- 1 medium yellow onion chopped
- 6 potatoes peeled and chopped
- 3 cups stock (vegetable beef or chicken)
- ½ teaspoon thyme
- 2 cups hot milk
- 1 cup hot heavy cream
- Salt and pepper

Prepare leeks by discarding dark green tops and outer leaves, then halve the light green and white parts lengthwise and cut into a half-moon shape rinse well under running water to remove hidden sand. In a large pot melt 2 tablespoons butter and then add leeks and onion. Sauté until onions are translucent. Add potatoes, stock, and thyme. Season with salt and pepper to taste. Bring to a boil, then reduce heat and simmer until potatoes are tender, 20 – 30 minutes. Add hot milk, stir well. Add hot cream and last tablespoon of butter.

**Tip: This soup is a chunky version of potato soup. This soup can be blended if you prefer a creamy soup. Also you can leave out the leeks and add 2 cups of sharp cheddar cheese for a delicious variation.

# White Onion Soup

The onion was considered a cure all by the Gaelic people. This soup in particular was used to cure colds and other ailments.

- 1 lb (3-4 medium) white onions – thinly sliced
- 3 tablespoons butter
- 2 tablespoons flour
- 3 cups chicken stock
- 1/8 teaspoon cloves
- 1 bay leaf
- 1 cup half and half
- Salt and pepper
- 2 oz Irish Whisky (optional)

Melt butter in a large pot. Add sliced onion and cloves. Sauté until soft but not browned! Sprinkle in flour and mix well. Cook 2 minutes and continue stirring. Add stock while continuing to stir. Add whisky if using. Add bay leaf and bring to a boil. Simmer 30 minutes stirring occasionally. Remove bay leaf. Gradually add half and half. Season with salt and pepper to taste. Heat through and serve.

☘ *Brotchan Roy*

This is one of Irelands oldest soup recipes. It is hearty, healthy, and very comforting.

- 5 medium leeks
- 3 tablespoons butter
- 5 tablespoons rolled oats
- 2 ¼ cups beef stock
- 2 cups half and half
- salt and pepper
- nutmeg

In a large pot melt butter add oats and cook until lightly browned. Gradually add the stock, bring to boil stirring constantly. Add sliced leeks. Season with salt and pepper to taste. Reduce heat and simmer slowly until thickened, 30 -40 minutes. Add half and half. Heat through. Remove from heat and let stand a few minutes before serving. Serve with a sprinkle of nutmeg if desired.

My Irish Nana,
Mary Harris Behrman

 ## *Pastina with Egg Broth*

- 4 cups chicken stock
- 2 eggs
- 4 tablespoons pecorino romano
- ½ cup pastina pasta
- ¼ teaspoon dry parsley
- salt and pepper to taste

Simmer stock until hot. Beat eggs in a small bowl. Add cheese, parsley and salt. Mix well. Cook pastina according to package in salted water to al dente. Drain and add to hot stock. Raise heat to bring stock to a boil. Dribble in the egg/cheese mixture and swirl with fork. Cook 1 minute and serve.

 ## *My Mama's Pastina al latte*

**'Pastina al latte' or pasta in milk is a close variation on the Pastina with Egg Broth recipe. Although it is not really a soup (unless you like a LOT of milk) it is so similar to the last recipe I added it to this section. My mother used to make the following recipe for me and my brother. It was our favorite "feel better" meal. Now, I make it for my children. Mom would also make this with no (or very little) milk and serve it as a side dish as well.

My brother Sean and I

- ½ cup pastina or orzo
- 1 cup milk - warmed
- 1 egg - beaten
- ½ cup pecorino romano

Cook pasta in salted water per package. Drain and immediately add the pasta and beaten egg back into the hot cook pot. Mix well. The hot pasta will cook the egg. Add warm milk and cheese as desired.

Tomato Bread Soup

A rustic, homey 'peasant' style soup. Great way to use up stale bread.

- 2 tablespoon olive oil
- 1 red onion chopped
- 3 cloves garlic minced
- 2 pounds very ripe tomatoes or 28oz canned plum tomatoes
- 4 cups chicken stock
- ½ teaspoon salt
- ¼ teaspoon red pepper
- ⅓ loaf stale Italian bread in 1" chunks
- Fresh basil chopped
- Italian parsley chopped

In a soup pot sauté onion and garlic in olive oil. If using fresh tomatoes plunge them into boiling water for 15 seconds, remove peel and chop. Add tomatoes, stock, salt, and red pepper to the pot. Simmer 15-20 minutes. Add bread chunks. Simmer 15 more minutes. Stir well. Remove from heat and add fresh herbs. Let stand 5 minutes and serve. It will be very thick – almost like a stew.

 ## *My Favorite Minestrone*

Traditionally minestrone is a vegetarian dish and is one of the best loved Italian soups. It is a great 'clean the fridge' or 'garden overabundance' soup. Make this one your own. This soup tastes better on day two, so consider making it the night before if possible.

- 3 tablespoons olive oil
- 1 onion, sliced
- 2 carrots, chopped
- 2 cloves of garlic minced
- 1 zucchini, thinly sliced
- 4 ounces green beans, cut into 1 inch pieces
- 2 stalks celery, thinly sliced
- 1 ½ quarts vegetable, chicken or beef stock
- 1 large can of diced tomatoes
- 3 potatoes – peeled and diced
- 1 tablespoon chopped fresh thyme or rosemary
- 1 (15 ounce) can cannellini beans, with liquid
- 1 chunk of Parmesan rind
- ¼ cup short cut pasta of your choice (optional)
- 4 cups baby spinach
- salt and ground black pepper to taste
- Parmesan cheese – grated for topping

Heat olive oil in a large saucepan over medium heat. Add onion, carrots, and garlic. Sauté for several minutes then add zucchini, green beans and celery. Cover, and reduce heat to low. Cook for 15 minutes, stirring occasionally. Stir in the stock, tomatoes, potatoes, Parmesan rind and herbs. Bring to a boil, replace the lid, and reduce heat to low; simmer gently for 30 minutes. Stir in the cannellini beans with liquid and pasta (if using). Simmer for an additional 10 minutes, or until pasta is al dente. Add the spinach. Remove the Parmesan rind. Season with salt & pepper.

 ## *Aunt Theresa's Pasta E Fagioli (Pasta and Beans)*

This is a hearty main dish soup. Delicious and nutritious comfort food. My husband's Great Aunt Theresa almost always had some cooking when we would visit.

- 3 garlic cloves minced
- 2 tablespoons olive oil
- 1 onion chopped
- 1 (16 oz) can plum tomatoes or 1 pound fresh plum tomatoes chopped
- 1 cup water or stock
- 1 (16oz) can cannellini beans
- ½ pound ditalini or elbows pasta or small shells
- ¼ tea crushed red pepper flakes
- salt and pepper
- grated cheese

My husband's Aunt Theresa and Uncle Tony.

In a large soup pot add olive oil and heat to medium. Add onions and garlic. Sauté until softened. Raise heat add beans, tomatoes, stock (or water), salt, pepper, red pepper. Bring to a boil. Reduce heat and simmer for 1 hour. In a second pot bring salted water to a boil add pasta and cook until al dente. Drain and add to the soup just before serving. Top with grated cheese if desired.

 ### *Easy Escarole Soup*

- 2 tablespoons olive oil
- 2 garlic cloves minced
- 1 onion chopped
- 1 potato peeled and diced small
- 2 cups chicken stock
- 2 heads of escarole washed and chopped

In large saucepan heat olive oil and gently cook garlic until lightly browned - be careful not to burn it. Add onion and potato. Then after a few minutes add the stock. Add escarole, cover and bring to a boil. Then lower heat and simmer at least an hour. The potato should have broken up and will help thicken the soup

My Mother, Doreen, and her sister Louise.

 ## Aunt Louise's Clams Oreganato

- 1 (6.5oz -10oz) can minced or chopped clams(drained reserve liquid)
- ¼ cup grated parmesan cheese
- ½ cup of seasoned bread crumbs
- 1 large garlic clove crushed and minced
- 1 teaspoon oregano
- paprika
- olive oil

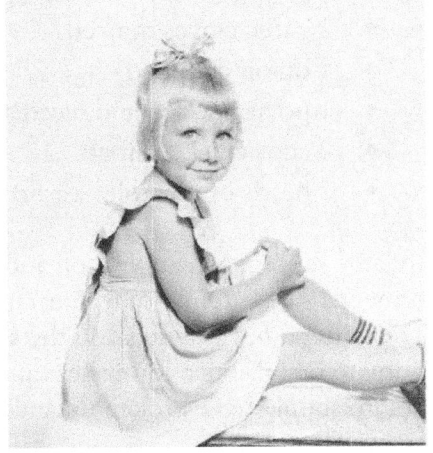

My Aunt (and Godmother) Louise

Clean, empty clam shells are traditionally used, but you can use any shallow oven proof container or just make into bite size patties.
Oil the clean clam shells and place on cookie sheet. Combine clams, garlic, breadcrumbs and cheese. Use reserved liquid 1 teaspoon at a time if mixture is dry and will not stick together. Press mixture into shells. Drizzle with olive oil, then sprinkle with oregano and paprika. Bake at 350° for 30 to 40 minutes. Or until lightly browned
Serve with lemon wedge if desired. .

 ## *Bruschetta*

Bruschetta means "little burnt ones" in Italian. These little grilled slices of country bread are tasty alone but are FANTASTIC when topped with whatever tidbits you can come up with, both sweet and savory. Use veggies, fruits, fish, meats, diced fresh tomatoes, figs and prosciutto, bean puree, thin seasoned slices of steak, or seared tuna. You are only limited by your imagination and taste. These can be carefully baked at 450° but grilling is best.

- thin country style Italian loaf
- extra virgin olive oil
- 2 whole garlic cloves peeled

Heat a grill pan. Slice the loaf of bread into ½ inch slices. Grill bread in a single layer until golden and crispy. Remove from grill and brush lightly with olive oil.
Rub garlic clove lightly over 1 side of toast. Top as desired.

Tip: Omit the garlic if you are looking for a sweet appetizer.

My husband's Maternal Grandparents – Irish Grandmother Helen, and Italian Grandfather Tony.

Mom's Stuffed Artichoke

My mother would make these on special occasions and I remember as a child thinking it was so much fun to pull the leaves between my teeth!

- 4 large whole artichokes
- ½ cup lemon juice
- 3 garlic cloves minced
- 4 tablespoons olive oil
- 2 cups seasoned bread crumbs
- 2 eggs
- ½ cup grated parmesan
- 1 cup chicken broth or stock
- olive oil for drizzle

Remove the stems from the artichokes so that they can stand up. Clean up any loose or damaged outer leaves. Lay artichoke on its side and cut 1 inch off the top of each one. Snip the tips of each leaf with scissors. Rub each artichoke with lemon juice. Place upside down in a large pot and add 3-4 cups of water, bring to a boil and simmer 10 minutes. Drain and cool. With a sharp knife trim away any prickly leaf tips that remain. Then pull out the bristly core of inner leaves to reveal the 'choke'. With a spoon, scoop out the hairy choke leaving the clean heart. Meanwhile in a large pan sauté garlic in the oil until lightly golden. Remove from heat. Add breadcrumbs, eggs, cheese, salt and pepper. Mix well. Stuff the artichoke centers and between the layers of leaves. Place upright in a baking pan. Add chicken broth to an and drizzle lightly with olive oil.
Cover and seal with foil and bake 45 minutes at 350°. Uncover and bake 20 more minutes serve hot or cold with wedges of lemon.
To eat these, pull off a leaf with some stuffing on the tip...place between your teeth and pull the leaf between your teeth until the inner stuffing covered tip comes off into your mouth. When the leaves are all gone, you can eat the delicious heart of the artichoke.

♣ *Pratie Oaten (Potato Cakes)*

These little potato cakes are an excellent addition to your breakfast plate but are equally good as an appetizer or party food. A swirl of sour cream and sprinkle of crispy bacon make a tasty appetizer. These also make a great addition to your Irish Fry!

- 2 cups mashed potatoes (no milk or butter just stiff mashed potatoes)
- 1 cup rolled oats
- 1 stick of butter
- salt and pepper

In a bowl combine potatoes and oats. Season well with salt and pepper. Add 2 tablespoons melted butter and stir to a firm, soft dough. You can add a little more oats if needed. Sprinkle counter with flour and roll dough out to about ½ inch thick. Cut into rounds (about a dozen) sprinkle tops with oats. Melt butter on a griddle or hot skillet. Add rounds and fry about 7 minutes per side or until golden. Serve hot with butter or sour cream.

** Tip: If making these as an appetizer or party food top with sour cream and a sprinkle of cheddar cheese and bacon, or chives, or some fried apples and onions, or whatever suits you.

Chapter 3 : Breads

Nothing beats the spirit-lifting aroma of baking bread. Most cultures and regions have some type of bread-centered traditions. Ireland and Italy are not exceptions.

Irelands breads are typically more simple and rustic. Simple or not they are both healthy and flavorful. The Emerald Isle is blessed with some very unique grains, and it also has a more limited selection of raw ingredients so the baking style and products there reflect this. Traditionally breads were baked near an open fire on a hearth stone or on a flat griddle called a Lec, which was hung above the embers. Bread was also baked in lidded cast iron pots that were buried in the embers. Many breads are sliced across the top to "let the fairies out".

In Italy, the importance of bread cannot be emphasized enough. Bread is practically revered and has been a part of every meal, on every table, rich or poor, since Roman times. There are many rituals involved in the baking and eating of bread in Italy. Bakers often make the sign of the cross over the oven, or cut it into the bread itself. If bread is dropped it must be immediately picked up and eaten because the waste of bread is said to doom you to purgatory.

🍀 Nana's Irish Soda Bread

- 4 cups flour
- 1 teaspoon baking soda
- 1 teaspoon baking powder
- ½ teaspoon salt
- 1 stick softened butter
- 1 ⅓ cups buttermilk
- 1 egg
- 2 tablespoons heavy cream
- raisins or caraway seed are optional....we prefer it plain usually.

Aunt Claire and Nana

Preheat oven to 375°
In a large bowl combine the first 5 ingredients with your hands, then mix in the buttermilk and egg. Work the mixture into a soft dough (folding in raisins or caraway if desired) Shape into a round loaf. Heavily grease a cookie sheet and set the loaf on it. Cut a shallow X in the top. Let rest 10-15 minutes. Brush top with the heavy cream and bake in preheated oven 1 hour or until done (hollow sounding when the bottom is tapped and golden brown.)

Tea Bannocks

- 2 cups all-purpose flour
- 1 cup old fashioned rolled oats
- $1/3$ cup brown sugar
- 1 tablespoon baking powder
- ½ teaspoon baking soda
- $3/4$ teaspoon salt
- 1 stick butter cold and cubed
- 1 large egg
- $2/3$ cup buttermilk

Preheat oven to 400°
Lightly flour a baking sheet
In the bowl of a food processor pulse flour, sugar, baking powder, baking soda, and salt with the cold butter until crumbly. Dump in a large bowl and stir in oats. In a small bowl whisk egg and buttermilk. Add to dry ingredients slowly, until well blended.. You need a soft moist ball (add additional buttermilk if needed.) with floured hands shape into 10" round about 1/2 inch thick on the prepared baking sheet. Bake 18 minutes or until browned and toothpick comes out clean. While warm, cut into wedges. Serve with lots of butter, marmalade and jam.

🍀 *Irish Buttermilk Bread*

- 2 cups flour
- 2 tablespoons wheat germ
- ½ teaspoon baking soda
- ½ teaspoon cream of tartar
- ½ teaspoon salt
- 1 teaspoon honey
- 1 tablespoon butter at room temp
- 1¾ tablespoons buttermilk

Hey, that's me at about 3years old making bread!

Preheat oven to 375°
Combine all dry ingredients in a large bowl. Cut in the butter until well combined. Add honey and buttermilk gradually blending until you have a sticky dough. Knead a few times to hold the dough together. Pat into a round and place on a cookie sheet or preheated baking stone. With a knife cut an X in the top of the loaf. Bake until golden brown about 30 minutes

Rosemary and Sea Salt Flatbread

- 1 package active dry yeast
- 1 ¼ cup warm water
- 3 ½ cups flour
- 3 tablespoons olive oil
- 1 teaspoon salt
- 2 tablespoons olive oil
- 2 tablespoons rosemary leaves finely chopped (fresh if available)
- 2 tablespoons coarse sea salt

In a small bowl dissolve yeast in ¼ cup warm water. Put flour and salt in a pile on a flat, floured surface. Make a well in the center and pour in dissolved yeast mixture. Mix together. If dough is too sticky sprinkle with a little more flour. When dough is formed knead for 10 minutes until smooth and elastic. Put dough in oiled bowl, turning to coat. Cover with a towel and let rise until double (about 1-2 hours). Preheat the oven to 425°

Punch down the dough and knead 5 times. Pat out dough into 2 oblongs about 1 inch thick. Using your fingertips back dents all over the surface of the surface of the dough. Brush with olive oil. Lay on a cookie sheet that has been sprinkled with cornmeal. Cover loosely with cling wrap and let rise about 30 minutes. Sprinkle liberally with sea salt and rosemary. Bake 25 minutes or until golden.

**TIP: Feel free to use other herbs, spices, or toppings (Olives? Caramelized onion? Sun dried tomatoes?) on this flatbread...there are many tasty combinations!

Tuscan Bread

Starter:
- 1 teaspoon active dry yeast
- $^2/_3$ cup warm water
- 1 ¼ cups white flour

Stir yeast into water and let stand 10 minutes. Add flour and stir to combine. Cover with plastic wrap let rise until tripled (about 6-8 hours)

- 1 ¼ active dry yeast
- $^1/_3$ cup warm water
- 1 cup water
- 2 $^2/_3$ cups white flour
- 1 cup whole wheat flour

Preheat over to 450°
Stir the yeast into the warm water and let sit 10 minutes. Add 1 cup of water to the starter and very well, break up the starter well (use your hands if needed) Stir in the flour mixture, a little at a time stirring well between additions. Sprinkle a little flour on your work surface and then knead dough until firm and elastic. Oil a large bowl and place dough in it and cover and let rise until double. Punch down and form into 2 oval loaves. Place on a lightly oiled baking sheet. Cover with a damp towel and let rise until doubled. Score the top of the loaves. Bake in a preheated 450° oven for 15 minutes then lower the oven to 400° and bake for an additional 25 minutes.

Italian Bread Bowls

These bread bowls are great to serve soups, stews or even chili in or fill with assorted hot and cold dips for your next party.

- 2 packages active dry yeast
- 2 ½ cups warm water
- 2 teaspoons salt
- 2 tablespoons vegetable oil
- 7 cups flour
- 1 tablespoon corn meal
- 1 egg white
- 1 tablespoon water

In a large bowl, dissolve yeast in warm water. Let stand until creamy, about 10 minutes.
Add salt, oil and 4 cups flour to the yeast mixture; mix well. Stir in the remaining flour, ½ cup at a time, mixing well with your hands or an electric mixer at medium speed after each addition.
When the dough comes together, turn it out onto a lightly floured surface and knead until smooth and elastic. Lightly oil a large bowl, place the dough in the bowl and turn to coat with oil. Cover with a damp cloth and let rise in a warm place until doubled. (about 1 hour)
Punch dough down, and divide into 8 equal portions. Shape each portion into a 4 inch round loaf. Place loaves on lightly greased baking sheets sprinkled with cornmeal. Cover and let rise in a warm place, free from drafts, until doubled (about 40 minutes).
Preheat oven to 400°. In a small bowl, beat together egg white and 1 tablespoon water; lightly brush the loaves with half of this egg wash. Bake in preheated oven for 15 minutes. Brush with remaining egg mixture, and bake 10 to 15 more minutes or until golden. Cool on wire racks.
To make bowls: Cut a 1/2 inch thick slice from top of each loaf; scoop out centers, leaving 3/4-inch-thick shells. Fill bread bowls with hot soup and serve immediately.

Mom's Italian Easter Egg Bread

- 2½ cups all-purpose flour, divided
- ¼ cup white sugar
- 1 teaspoon salt
- 1package package active dry yeast
- $^2/_3$ cup milk
- 2 tablespoons butter
- 2 eggs
- ½ teaspoon anise seed (optional)
- ½ cup mixed candied fruit (optional)
- 5 whole eggs, dyed if desired
- 2 tablespoons butter, melted

Combine milk and butter and anise seed (if using) in a small saucepan; heat until milk is warm and butter is softened but not melted. In a large bowl, combine 1 cup flour, sugar, salt and yeast; stir well. Gradually add the milk and butter to the flour mixture; stirring constantly. Add 2 eggs and ½ cup flour; beat well. Add the remaining flour and candied fruit (if using) stirring well. When the dough has pulled together, turn it out onto a lightly floured surface and knead until smooth and elastic.

Lightly oil a large bowl, place the dough in the bowl and turn to coat with oil. Cover with a damp cloth and let rise in a warm place until

My Father's Sisters, Claire and Barbara

doubled in volume.

NOTE: I heat the oven to about 200° then turn it off. This makes a warm draft free place to let your bread rise.

Punch down the dough. Turn it out onto a lightly floured surface. Let dough rest 10 minutes. Divide dough into 6 sections. Take 5 sections and divide into 3 ropes. Braid the ropes into a small wreath pinching ends together. Nest the colored egg snuggly in the center of the bread. Do this 5 times. The 6th section is used to roll out a 'cross' to lay over each egg (an optional step if you don't do the crosses just add the 6th section into the braid!) Pinch to seal. Cover and let rise again. Bake at 350° for about 35minutes or until golden brown.

Tip: I never add the candied fruit...I don't like it. But feel free to experiment. I like anise, but some in my family don't so that is something I add only on occasion.

Rustic Italian Bread

- 1 cup warm water
- 3 cups all-purpose flour
- 2 teaspoons granulated sugar
- 1 teaspoon salt2 ½ teaspoons of active dry yeast
- 1 tablespoon of olive oil
- 1 tablespoon of sea salt or sesame seeds

Preheat your oven to 375° degrees In a bowl, add 1 cup of warm water and dry active yeast and let it stand until creamy (about 5 minutes). In another bowl add flour, salt, and sugar. After 5 minutes take the yeast and give it a gentle stir. Then add it to the flour mixture, mixing it in with a fork until sticky. Sprinkle with a bit more flour and work it with your hands to make a ball. Take the dough and gently mold it into a smooth but firm ball with an elastic feel. Put the dough back into the bowl and cover with a kitchen towel and let it rise. This could take anywhere from 30 minutes to 1 hour. At this point punch down the dough and roll it into a ball again. Put the dough back into the bowl and let it rise 1 more time.

After the bread has risen for the second time, take the dough and put it on the parchment paper that is on a cookie sheet. Shape dough into an oval. Take about 1 tablespoon of olive oil and coat the dough with it and sprinkle a bit of sea salt or sesame seeds on top. Score the top of the dough with a sharp knife at a 45 degree angle. Bake 30 minutes, until you hear a hollow sound when you tap the bottom. Allow the bread to cool slightly before serving.

My Nana and Great-Great Grandmother

Chapter 4 : Sides

What are side dishes really but the "accessories" that bring together the meal? I mean turkey at Thanksgiving might be the main dish but is Thanksgiving really Thanksgiving without the sides? The stuffing and the mashed potatoes? Of course not! So don't let your side dishes be an afterthought.

♣ Honeyed Parsnips

- 8 medium parsnips peeled and thick sliced
- 4 tablespoons oil
- 2 tablespoons honey

Preheat oven to 350°. Boil the sliced parsnips about 5 minutes and drain well. Pour ½ the oil in a baking dish. Add parsnips.
In a small bowl, whisk remaining oil and honey. Drizzle evenly over parsnips. Roast in oven 45 minutes or until golden and tender.

**Tip: This recipe also works with fresh carrots!

My Dad, James

☘ *Baked Leeks and Cream*

- 8 medium leeks
- salt and pepper
- 1 ¼ cup milk
- 10 slices of crispy bacon crumbled
- 1 egg
- ²/₃ cup cream
- 1 tablespoon stone ground mustard
- ¾ cup shredded sharp Irish Cheddar cheese

Slice leeks into large chunks and rinse well. Season with salt and pepper add to saucepan. Add milk and simmer 2 minutes. Drain. Put leeks in a buttered baking dish. Sprinkle the bacon over the leeks. In a saucepan blend egg, cream, and mustard. Heat slowly over low heat – DO NOT BOIL. Stir often until slightly thickened. Taste, and season if needed. Pour over leeks. Sprinkle with cheese. Bake at 350° for 10 minutes or until cheeses is melted and bubbly.

☘ *Colcannon and Champ*

Both of these dishes are VERY traditional Irish dishes. Nowadays Colcannon is most often made with potato and cabbage but kale can also be used. This dish is often thought of as interchangeable with Champ. Although they are both a mashed potato dish, Colcannon is equal parts potatoes and greens, while Champ is a mashed potatoes dish that is flavored with flecks of green onions and/or fresh herbs.

Colcannon

- 1 lb potatoes – peeled
- 1 lb cabbage or kale shredded
- ½ cup hot milk or cream
- 4+ tablespoons butter
- salt and pepper

Cover potatoes with cold salted water. Bring to a boil, reduce heat and simmer until tender. With a slotted spoon, transfer the potatoes to a large bowl and mash with 2-3 tablespoons butter. In the hot potato water cook the cabbage(or kale) until tender but crisp. Drain and add to the hot potatoes. Add hot milk(or cream) and additional 1-2 tablespoons butter. Season and mix together well. Serve mounded on the plate with a 'well' in the center. Fill the well with melted butter for dipping the Colcannon.

Champ

- 1 ½ lb potatoes – peeled
- 1 bunch green onions
- 1 ¼ cups milk
- fresh chives and/or parsley (optional)
- salt and pepper
- butter

Boil potatoes in salted water until tender. Drain. Return to the pot. In a smaller pan boil the green onion in the milk for 5 minutes. Beat the potato with the boiled milk and green onion. Keep potato pan on a very low heat while you beat the potatoes. Add additional milk if needed until potatoes are creamy. Season with salt and pepper. Stir in chopped herbs if using. Serve hot with a large dollop of butter.

Creamy Polenta with Cheese

- 4 cups of water
- 1 cup yellow cornmeal (polenta)
- ½ teaspoon salt
- ¹/₃ cup grated parmesan
- salt and pepper
- 2 oz sharp provolone shredded (optional)
- ¼ cup cream

In a large saucepan heat water over medium heat. Slowly stir in polenta. Stir continuously while pour to avoid lumps. Stir the pot almost constantly for 45 minutes or until polenta is thickened and comes away from the side of the pan while stirring. Remove from heat and stir in parmesan (and provolone if using) season and stir until cheese is melted and combined. Stir in cream. Serve hot and creamy as a side or as a bed for meats or sautéed veggies.

**TIP: To make chilled polenta which you can slice and fry or broil – omit the cream. Make polenta the same as above then turn hot polenta out onto a wooden cutting board and spread to a ½ inch thickness. Cool completely. Cut into slices. These can be fried in olive oil until golden or broiled on each side until browned.

Fried Potatoes and Peppers

- 4 medium russet potatoes
- 2 large green bell peppers
- 2 large red peppers
- 4 tablespoons olive oil
- 1 large onion
- salt and pepper

Wash peel and slice potatoes. Wash and slice peppers into strips, slice onion into thin strips.
In a large skillet heat half of the oil. Sauté onion until soft. Then remove from pan. Add potatoes, tossing in oil to coat.
Fry potatoes until olden brown, turning as needed. Remove from pan. Add remaining oil and add the peppers.
Stir to coat in oil then sauté until lightly browned.
Return onions and potatoes to the skillet. Season.
Lower heat and cook 10 minutes until all are tender.

Insalata Caprese

Super simple perfection! The only thing you need to remember is this is a 'seasonal' dish. Summer ripened tomatoes and good quality fresh mozzarella are a must.

- ½ pound fresh mozzarella cheese (buffalo if you can get it) sliced ¼-inch thick
- 2 large vine-ripened tomatoes, sliced ¼-inch thick
- 1 cup fresh basil leaves
- sea salt to taste
- freshly-ground black pepper to taste
- ¼ cup extra-virgin olive oil

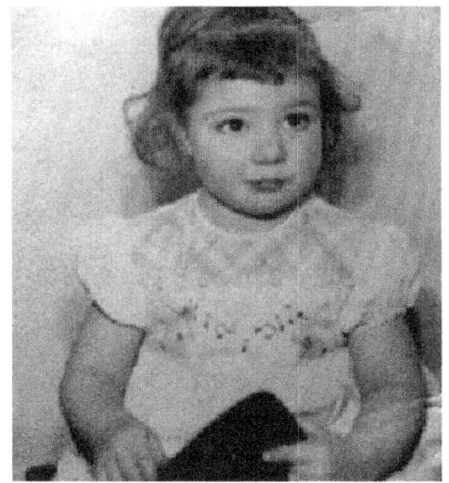

My Mother, Doreen

In a circular design around the side of a serving plate, alternate fresh mozzarella slices on a large platter (or on individual plates if you are doing individual portions) with sliced tomatoes and a basil leaf, overlapping for effect.

Add salt and freshly ground pepper to taste. Just before serving, lightly drizzle on some top-quality extra-virgin olive oil.

Chapter 5 : Entree

The main course... the part of the meal that all other components should compliment. The Star of the show, so to speak. This chapter is the heart of the meal you are serving and as such should be warm and generous. It should make you feel happy and satisfied.

Saltimbocca

- 8 veal cutlets (scaloppini if you can find it)
- sea salt
- cracked black pepper
- 16-20 fresh sage leaves
- 8 slices of prosciutto
- ½ cup flour
- 1 stick of butter
- 1 cup white wine

Place slices of veal between 2 pieces of cling wrap and pound thin, about ¼ inch. Season with salt and pepper. Place 1 slice of prosciutto and a few sage leaves on the cutlet. Roll up over the prosciutto and sage and secure with a toothpick.

My Mom and Dad

In a bowl season the flour with salt and pepper. Coat each roll-up in the seasoned flour. In a skillet melt butter. Cook veal in batches browning all sides. Keep cooked veal warm under foil. When the veal is all cooked and covered. Deglaze the pan with the wine. Scrap the bits from the bottom of the pan and reduce by half. Pour over veal and serve.

**Tip: This dish is also delicious when made with Chicken cutlet instead of veal.

☘ Dublin Coddle

This is one of Dublin's oldest dishes, traditionally eaten when the men folk came home from the pub on a Saturday night. The term 'coddle' simply means slow cooked.

- 1 ½ pounds of pork sausage cut into chunks
- 1 ½ pounds of bacon cut into pieces –(smoked ham can be substituted)
- 1 quart of water
- 1 tablespoon olive oil
- 2 large sweet onions sliced
- 2 pounds of potatoes peeled and sliced thickly
- salt
- pepper
- fresh parsley

Preheat oven to 350°
Put sausage, bacon(or ham) and water in a pot and boil 5 minutes covered. Drain and reserve the liquid. In a large skillet brown meats in oil. Put meats in a greased casserole dish. Add onions and potatoes and season with salt and pepper. Add enough of the reserved liquid to cover.
Cover casserole dish and bake for at least 1 hour. Test potatoes for doneness, and add a little water or reserved liquid if needed.
Remove the cover during the last ½ hour.
Serve with soda bread.

Mom's Braciole

My mother makes this dish whenever she cooks up a batch of sauce (or gravy as she calls it!) No matter what she is doing with the sauce, plain, meatballs, or sausages, she generally throws at least one Braciole in the sauce while it cooks. She also swears by Locatelli cheese which is a specific brand of pecorino romano.

- 1 lb thin round steak. - about 2-3 pieces
- ½ cup Italian flavored bread crumbs
- ½ cup Locatelli grated cheese (pecorino romano)
- ¼ grated provolone
- 1 – 2 eggs
- 3 tablespoons of olive oil
- 2 cloves garlic crushed
- 2 quarts or so of your favorite tomato Sauce

Simmer tomato sauce. Mix cheeses, bread crumbs and 1 egg to form a wet paste (add 2nd egg if needed.) Spread equal portions over the steaks. Roll each steak tightly over filling and secure with butcher's twine. Heat olive oil in a pan with the garlic. Remove the garlic once it is very lightly browned. Brown the meat on all sides. When all the meat is browned place the braciole into the sauce and simmer for 2 hours.

🍀 *Fish Cakes*

Fish Cakes have always been a popular way to serve fish, especially to children. They have over time also become a popular pub food. Simple and easy to prepare these little cakes are delicious!

- 1 pound of smoked haddock
- 4 tablespoons butter
- 2 tablespoons lemon juice
- 1 pound potatoes – cooked and cubed
- 2 teaspoons lemon zest
- 1 egg
- salt and pepper
- 3 tablespoons flour
- salt and pepper
- 1 egg - beaten
- ¼ cup seasoned breadcrumbs
- oil for frying

My Great Grandfather Jacob, his sister Anna, and my great-great grandparents.

Butter an oven proof dish with 2 tablespoons butter. Lay fish fillets over butter cover lightly with foil and bake at 350 for 15 minutes. Cool, pick fish carefully looking for bones. Mixing fish into the mashed potatoes and season with salt, pepper and zest. Let the mixture set until cold, then mix in egg. Divide mixture and make 8 patties. Mix flour, salt and pepper on a plate, lightly coat each patty. Then dip each patty into beaten egg, and finally into the breadcrumbs. Fry in hot oil until golden and warmed through. Drain on paper towels. Serve warm.

Irish Fry

'The Fry' is one of Irelands most well-known dishes. It is eaten (with a great many variations) in most home across Ireland. Although it resembles an American breakfast, the Fry is eaten at any time of the day. When eaten in the morning the Fry tends to be a little less hearty. Later day meals tend to add some steak or liver to the mix. Here is a general Irish Fry (I don't add black or white pudding because I don't like it but feel free if you do) This recipe is for 1 or 2 servings.

- 2 thick slices of bacon
- 2 sausage links
- 2 slices of white or black pudding (optional)
- ½ a farl of soda bread (a farl is a piece of round soda bread that is cut into 4 triangular pieces)
- 1 potato cake
- 1 or 2 eggs
- 4 tablespoons lard or oil

Be sure to cook your fry in the right order so you can serve everything on one plate at the same time.

In a pan, fry the sausages in a little oil or lard over a gentle heat until cooked through. Increase the heat and add the bacon. Fry until bacon is beginning to crisp and the sausages are browned. Remove them from the pan and drain on paper towels – keep warm. Fry pudding slices if using and add them to the warm dish with the other meats. Cut the farl and potato cake in half and fry in the bacon/sausage fat until crisped (add more lard or oil if needed) Remove and keep warm. Add any remaining lard/oil to pan and heat. Crack egg into the melted fat/oil. Tip pan and spoon some hot oil over the top of the egg(s), cooking the top of the egg. When egg is cooked how you like arrange all components on a plate and serve. The Fry is traditionally with a strong tea.

♣ MaryJo's Boiled Dinner

- 1 smoked ham shoulder (bone in) 3 lbs
- 4 carrots, cut into 1-inch pieces
- 1 small cabbage, chopped coarsely
- 4 medium potatoes, peeled and cut into 1-inch pieces
- 1 onion, diced
- 1 bay leaf
- 8 cups water or enough to cover ham 1"
- $1/_8$ cup cider vinegar (plus more when serving)
- salt and pepper to taste

Combine ham, carrot, onion, potato and bay leaf in a stock pot with water and bring to a boil then cover and simmer for about 2-3 hours or until ham in tender. Add cabbage and vinegar in the last 20 minutes. Serve with a splash (or more) of vinegar if desired.

My Mother in Law, MaryJo Parente Schweiger

***Tip: This dish can also be made with corned beef!

Slow Cooker Italian Sandwiches

Well don't you sometimes just feel like a zesty drippy hot sandwich? Come on you know you do. Oh...and there needs to be some melted cheese and a crusty yet soft roll too now doesn't there? Well here is an easy way to get just such a sandwich!

- 1 boneless chuck roast (4lbs)
- 1 jar pepperoncini
- 1 can beef broth
- 1 bottle dark beer or ale
- 1 onion diced
- 3 tablespoons Italian Herb Blend
- your favorite bread or rolls
- slices of sharp provolone or Gouda

Trim Roast. Place in crockpot. Drain (save juices) and chop pepperoncini .

Add chopped pepperoncini and 3 Tablespoons (or more if you like the heat) of juices to the crock pot. Add next 4 ingredients.

Cover and cook on low 8 hours or until you can "pull" or shred the meat.

Remove meat from pot and shred..

Return to the cooker and let soak in juices until ready to serve.

Serve on rolls with cheese and any other toppings(lettuce, tomato, etc) that you like. Enjoy!!

Beef Stew in Stout

My family loves this. It is a comforting, hearty, soul soothing dish. I always use Guinness Stout when I make this stew and it adds the perfect depth and taste and is the most traditionally Irish choice of stout there is. This stew goes terrific with dumplings if that is your thing. Or serve it up with hunks of fresh bread and enjoy! Although I usually cook this in the oven, it comes out great in the crock pot too!

- 3 tablespoons oil
- 2 large yellow onions sliced
- 8 large carrots peeled and sliced
- 4 large potatoes peeled cut into a small cube
- 6 – 8 tablespoons flour
- 1 tablespoon cracked black pepper
- ½ teaspoon salt
- 3 pound stew meat cubed
- 1 ½ bottles of Guinness Stout
- 1 teaspoon brown sugar
- 2 bay leaves
- 2 teaspoons fresh thyme chopped
- ½ - 1 cup beef stock

Preheat your oven to 325°.

In an oven proof covered casserole add 1 tablespoon oil and potatoes. Cook 5 minutes stirring. Add onions and carrots. Cook on stove over low heat until onions are softened. In a Ziploc bag place flour, cracked pepper, and ½ teaspoon salt. Add beef in batches, close and shake bag to coat beef. Remove veggies from the pan add 2 tablespoons oil. Brown beef in batches. When all of the beef is browned return everything to the casserole. Sprinkle with any remaining flour. Sprinkle sugar over all. Add thyme and bay leaves. Pour stout over all. Add ½ - 1 cup beef stock. Bring to a boil. Cover then place in preheated oven and cook for 2 hours. Remove lid to help thicken during last ½ hour if needed.

Linguini and White Clam Sauce

- 2 pounds linguini
- $1/3$ cup olive oil
- 8 cloves of garlic sliced as thin as possible
- 1 or 2 (7oz) jars of Italian baby clams rinsed well (I like a lot of clams!)
- ½ cup of bottled of clam juice
- 1 teaspoon red pepper flakes(optional)
- sea salt
- percorino romano grated cheese (optional)

Cook linguini according to package directions in salted water.

Heat olive oil and garlic over low to medium heat until garlic is soft but not browned. Add clams and cook for 1 minute. Add clam juice and cook 2 minutes. When linguini is done drain and add pasta to the pan with the sauce. Toss well to coat. Season as desired with red pepper flakes, sea salt and grated cheese.

My Grandparents, Mom, Aunt and Uncles.

Kelly's Italian Style Macaroni and Cheese

- 1 pound short cut pasta of your choice (I like shells)
- 1 cup diced pancetta
- ½ cup chopped oil packed sun-dried tomatoes
- 2 cloves garlic minced
- ½ cup roasted red peppers peppers, diced
- 1 medium yellow onion, diced
- 2 tablespoons butter
- 3 tablespoons all-purpose flour
- 2 cups milk
- ½ cup heavy cream
- 1 cup shredded fontina cheese
- 1 cup shredded sharp provolone cheese
- ½ cup pecorino romano cheese grated (separated)
- ¼ cup shredded fresh basil
- salt and black pepper, to taste

Bring a large saucepan of salted water to a boil. Cook pasta according to package directions. Drain and set aside.

Meanwhile, in a large saucepan over medium-high, sauté the pancetta until crisped and browned, about 5 minutes. Add the sun-dried tomatoes, red peppers and onion. Continue to cook until the onion is very tender, about 5 to 6 minutes. Then add garlic and cook several minutes more until fragrant. Be very careful not to burn the garlic as it will become bitter. Add the butter and stir until melted. Add the flour and stir to coat well.

Pour in the milk. Bring the mixture to a boil, add the cream, and return to boil continuing to stir. Cook until thickened. Turn off the heat and stir in the fontina, provolone, and ½ of the pecorino romano. Stir until all of the cheese has melted. Stir in the basil and the cooked pasta. Season with salt and black pepper. Pour into a baking dish that has been sprayed with cooking spray (or buttered if you prefer). Sprinkle with remaining pecorino romano and bake at 350° uncovered until cheese on top is melted and slightly golden.

Aunt Mary's Semolina Pasta

My Aunt Mary (great-aunt actually) is a wonderful woman. Originally from Southern Italy (the 'heel of the boot' as she says!) This is her recipe (well according to her it is NOT her recipe it is just "the way we did things…there is no recipe")

- 2 cups all-purpose flour
- 2 cups semolina flour
- 1 pinch salt
- 6 large eggs
- 2 tablespoons olive oil

Thoroughly sift together all-purpose flour, semolina flour, and pinch of salt. On a clean surface, make a mountain out of flour mixture then make a deep well in center. Break the eggs into the well and add olive oil. Whisk eggs very gently with a fork, gradually incorporating flour from the sides of the well. When mixture becomes too thick to mix with a fork, begin kneading with your hands.

Great-Aunt Mary Costantini

Knead dough for 8 to 12 minutes, until it is smooth and supple. Dust dough and work surface with semolina or flour as needed to keep dough from becoming sticky. Wrap dough tightly in plastic and allow it to rest at room temperature for 30 minutes.

Roll out dough with a pasta machine or a rolling pin to desired thickness. Cut into your favorite style of noodle or stuff with your favorite filling to make ravioli. Bring water to a boil in a large pot, and then add 4 tablespoons salt. Cook pasta until tender 3-5 minutes. Top with your favorite sauce and enjoy!

Aunt Linda's Sunday Gravy

- olive oil
- 2 cans (28oz) of tomatoes Puree with basil
- 1 can (28oz) tomatoes whole, with basil -crushed with your hands
- 1 can (14.5oz) fire-roasted tomatoes
- 10 cloves of garlic -smacked and minced well
- 12 -15 small homemade uncooked meatballs
- 1 lb Italian sweet sausage- cut bite size
- 1 lb Italian hot sausage -cut bite size
- pepper
- sugar (optional - start with a few tablespoons)
- fresh basil

In a very large pot, coat bottom with a few glugs of olive oil(3-4 Tablespoon to start add more if needed). Sauté garlic until fragrant (do NOT brown it). Add to the garlic and olive oil the pureed tomatoes. Then add the crushed whole tomatoes and the fire-roasted tomatoes. Simmer on low. In a large skillet, add a few glugs of olive oil and brown the sausage- then remove from pan and put into the tomato mixture. Now fry meatballs in the same pan(do not wipe out or rinse the pan). When the meatballs are brown, put them and all of the flavorful crusty bits and any oil left in the pan right into the sauce. Simmer at least 2 hours, but you could simmer it all day. Add water (or tomato puree) if it gets to thick (or even a splash of red wine) Taste and season. If it seems acidic add the sugar. Just before serving chop or julienne the basil and throw it into the pot and stir through.

Aunt Linda's Meatballs

- 1 lb ground beef
- 2 eggs
- ¼ cup Italian flavored bread crumbs
- 1 – 1 ½ cups locatelli grated cheese (pecorino romano)
- salt and pepper
- 3 tablespoons olive oil

Aunt Linda Bernitt

Mix all of the ingredients together, first with a fork and then with wet hands. Mix until you have a nice smooth consistency. Then roll into balls. You should get 10 or 11 medium sized meatballs. Lightly sauté the meatballs in olive oil but do not cook them through. Add them to your favorite sauce and simmer while your sauce cooks. Meatballs will finish cooking in the sauce.

Vodka Sauce

- 1 tablespoon butter
- 1 tablespoon olive oil
- 3 cloves garlic minced
- 1 ¼ cups vodka
- 1 can (28oz) crushed tomatoes
- 1 can (14.5 oz) diced tomatoes with fennel and red pepper
- sea salt and cracked black pepper to taste
- ½ cup heavy cream
- ½ cup fresh basil leaves

Heat a large skillet, heat butter and oil over medium heat, add garlic cook 1-2 minutes until fragrant but do not brown.
Pour in vodka. Bring mixture to a boil and cook over medium heat until reduced by half, about 4 minutes.
Add tomatoes return to boil. Reduce and simmer about 10 minutes. season to taste with salt and pepper. Remove from heat add cream and basil. Stir gently and toss with pasta of your choice.

Nana's Kidney Stew over Noodles

The Irish tend to make use of the whole animal, organs included. This recipe is time consuming (2 days) and day 1 is not overly pleasant. My Nana made this dish the first time my Dad brought his new girlfriend (my 14 year old mother) home for dinner. My poor Italian Mother! She was scared to death to try it, but she loved it and 51 years later makes it several times a year as a treat for my Dad. The gravy is thick and rich. Beef kidneys are not easy to come by, so if you like it make a big batch and freeze the extras. I personally do not make this dish, so this recipe is straight from my Nana to my Mom to you all!

- 4 beef kidneys
- ½ lbs fatty bacon
- 2 large onions
- 2 tablespoons kitchen bouquet
- ¼ cup (ish) flour
- salt and pepper
- 8 ounce bag egg noodles

Day 1: Wash the kidneys well in cold water. Cut each kidney in half along fatty part. Put is a stock pot and cover with cold water. Bring to a slow boil, then lower heat and simmer for 4 - 6 hours. Don't be alarmed if it smells bad - they are supposed to! This is one reason the kidneys are not served the day they are boiled.
Skim off any foam and discard. You will need to skim this several times as it cooks. Drain and save any clear broth. Discard any sediment or foam. Set aside the broth.
When the kidneys are cool enough cut into bite-size pieces removing ALL fat. Put pieces in a bowl, cover with some of the broth so the meat is all covered. Cover the bowl tightly and put in the refrigerator overnight. Refrigerate the rest of the broth as well.

Day 2: Remove the kidneys and broth from the refrigerator and set aside. Cut bacon into bite size pieces and dice onions. Brown over low heat in a skillet. When the bacon is browned and the onions are soft remove them to a bowl. Whisk the flour a few tablespoons at a time into the hot bacon drippings. Keeping pan over medium heat, slowly add the broth while whisking to make a gravy. As the gravy thickens season with salt and pepper, add kitchen bouquet. Add bacon and onion to the gravy. Add kidneys. Prepare the egg noodles per the package instructions. Heat kidneys/gravy until nice and hot. Serve over the egg noodles.

Nana, Aunt Claire, Aunt Barbara, and my Dad.

Chapter 6 : Desserts and Treats

Dessert. What more do you need to say? That perfect ending to a perfect meal. Or maybe you are just craving a sweet something to lift your spirit? Or maybe a spirit to lift your spirits?

Grandma's Italian Bowtie Cookies

Not very sweet, a tad bit addicting, these traditional Italian cookies were always one of my Mom's favorites and I remember helping her "tie" these when I was younger. They are a perfect little "something" to snack on with your coffee or tea. They are not at all what we Americans think of as a cookie, but like I said they are tasty! This is my grandmother's recipe. My grandmother loved to bake. She always tried to remember everyone's favorites and bake them when they came to visit. So cook up a batch of these, call a friend, put on a pot of tea or coffee and visit for awhile.

- 2 eggs
- 2 tablespoons sugar
- 2 cups sifted flour
- 2 tablespoons vanilla (I add a touch more)
- Oil for frying
- Powdered sugar

Beat together the eggs and sugar in a medium size bowl until the mixture is light and fluffy. Stir in 1 ½ cup of the flour & the vanilla until blended. Shape into a ball.
Turn the dough out onto lightly floured surface. Knead until the dough is smooth and elastic, about 8 minutes; add as much of the remaining flour as necessary to prevent sticking. Cover with plastic wrap. Let rest 5 minutes.
Divide dough into 4 equal portions. Roll ¼ of the dough to ⅛ inch thickness. Keep remaining dough covered with plastic wrap while working with the one fourth. Cut into 5 x 1 ½ inch strips with pastry wheel or pizza cutter. Make a lengthwise slit about 1 inch long in center of each strip. Pull one end through the slit to make a bowtie. As you work, keep bowties covered with plastic wrap. Repeat with remaining dough.
Pour oil into large fry pan or deep fryer to a depth of 4 inches. Heat oil until it registers 375° on a deep fat frying thermometer.

Fry a few cookies at a time for a total of 3 minutes or until golden brown, turning once.
Drain on paper toweling; cool.
Fry remaining cookies in small batches.
Store cooled cookies in tightly covered containers.
Sprinkle with powdered sugar just before serving.
Makes about 2 dozen

The Italian Side in NYC

Nevatels

There is a funny family story about this recipe. One day Great Grandma was at home in her kitchen in the Bronx NY with a couple of her neighbor friends. They were having some coffee and Great Grandma served up her pastries. One of her friends said, " Eh Luiza...whatsa in thisa pastry? " To which she replied ...."AAAh'll neva tell." So it came to be whenever these wonderful delights are served we call them NEVATELS.

- 1 ½ cups Hershey's syrup
- 1 ½ cups chopped walnuts
- 1 ½ cups chopped raisins
- 1 cup chopped dried fruit and peel (I pick out the green ones I don't like them)
- a handful of chopped pignoli (pine nuts)
- 4 piecrusts --- either homemade or Boxes of Pillsbury pie crusts -which I roll out thinner (my preference)

I like my circles to be around 3 inches across, use a small dish as a measure.
Mix all the ingredients, if it seems a little dry add more chocolate syrup. If it's too wet it will leak all out of the dough.
Put a couple of spoonfuls in each circle and fold over into a half moon. seal edges
Bake at 400° for 12-15 minutes.
Yields about 40 pastries.

I added a quick recipe for homemade Chocolate syrup! Just in case you did not have any on hand and were craving a Nevatel!

Chocolate Syrup

- 1¼ cups sugar
- 1 cup unsweetened cocoa powder
- 1 cup water
- ¼ teaspoon salt
- 2 teaspoons vanilla extract

Whisk together 1st 4 ingredients well. Bring to a boil, stirring all the time. When it reaches a boil reduce heat and simmer until slightly thickened. Whisk in vanilla.
Cool for 5 - 10 minutes
Store in the refrigerator

Frank and Luiza Costantini

Grandma's Struffoli

- 6 eggs
- 1 cup granulated sugar
- 2 sticks of butter room temp
- 4 ½ cups all-purpose flour
- 1 teaspoon vanilla
- 2 tablespoons baking powder
- 1 teaspoon salt
- vegetable oil for frying
- 1 lb honey
- 1 teaspoon lemon or orange zest (optional)
- 1 small jar multi-color candy sprinkles

Whisk eggs very well. Beat sugar into eggs. In a large bowl combine flour, baking powder, and salt. Rub butter into the flour with your hands.

Add vanilla to the sugar/egg mixture. Put mixture the into a mixer and mix (using dough hook) and slowly add the flour/butter mixture. Let dough rest in a cool dry place for at least 30 minutes.

Divide dough into fourths. Roll out the dough in sections. Cut dough into ½-inch strips and cut ½inch pieces from the strips. Make each ½-inch piece into balls about the size of a hazelnut. Place the ball onto a baking pan.

Put vegetable oil into a large pot and bring to 350° Fry small quantities of the dough balls in the oil and when golden brown, place onto a baking pan lined with paper towels to absorb excess oil. When all dough is fried, let cool to room temperature.

In a saucepan, heat the honey and zest if using (not to a boil) and add small quantities of the fried dough to the pan. Stir lightly with a large slotted spoon. Remove from saucepan and place onto a serving plate. Mound the honey covered balls into a pile in the center of the plate and sprinkle with candy sprinkles.

🍀 Nana's Baked Rice Pudding

- 2 tablespoons uncooked rice
- 2 cups whole milk
- ¼ teaspoon salt
- ¼ cup sugar
- ½ teaspoon vanilla
- ½ teaspoon grated lemon peel
- nutmeg (optional)
- heavy cream (optional)
- butter

Preheat oven to 275°.
Mix rice, milk, salt, sugar , vanilla, and lemon peel. After it is mixed well and the sugar is dissolved, pour into a generously buttered baking dish.
Bake for about 3hours or until set, stirring several times during the 1st hour only!
Serve warm with nutmeg and a drizzle of heavy cream.

My Nana Mary

♣ Bread and Butter Pudding

My husband loves comfort food, warm, homey, rich, old-fashioned comfort food. This recipe is classic comfort food. It is divine, especially when it is a little chilly and you want something to warm you body and soul. It is easy to make and is best when served warm from the oven with cream poured over it. (hey …I never said it was low-fat or anything!)

This is an excellent way to use up slightly stale white bread. You can also make it a million different ways by using different breads, rolls, croissants, Panetonne, Brioche, cinnamon raisin bread.

While the measurements here are "loose" - because it is a sort of carefree type recipe - you definitely MUST use whole milk and heavy cream to make it properly. You also want to butter your bread liberally. We are looking for comfort food not calorie counting. So if your bread slices are bigger or smaller…you may need more or less butter…this is fine and it won't hurt the recipe a bit. Oh, and if you don't like raisins…leave them out or add one of your favorites dried fruits (currents, dried cherries, figs) or maybe even chocolate chips.

- 2 sticks of butter soft
- 12 slices of slightly stale bread (you CAN use fresh but the stale soaks up the custard better)
- 1 ½ cups whole milk
- 1 ½ cups heavy cream
- 8 egg yolks
- 1 teaspoon vanilla
- ¾ cup sugar
- ¼ cup golden raisins and regular raisins combined

Combine milk and whipping cream in heavy large saucepan, add vanilla.. Bring milk mixture to simmer.
Whisk egg yolks and ¾ cup sugar in large bowl to blend.
Very, very gradually whisk hot milk mixture into yolk mixture (start with a few tablespoons at a time and KEEP whisking…you don't want scrambled eggs!).

Set custard aside.
Butter a glass baking dish. Spread butter over both sides of bread slices. Arrange some bread slices in single layer over bottom of prepared dish, trimming to fit. Sprinkle half of golden raisins and half of brown raisins over bread.
Cover with another single layer of buttered bread. Sprinkle remaining raisins over. Layer with the remaining bread. Pour milk mixture over bread.
Let stand until most of the custard is absorbed, about 20-30 minutes. Position rack in center of oven and preheat to 325°.
Bake pudding until custard thickens and begins to set, about 20-40 minutes. There is a big difference in time because it will depend on the type of bread and how many layers you did.

If you prefer a less sweet pudding simply skip the following step
Sprinkle with a few tablespoons of sugar and broil VERY CAREFULLY until the pudding begins to brown slightly.
Be careful as it is very easy to burn the top.
Serve warm.

Tip: Serve with ice cream, or in a bowl drizzled with heavy cream.

Aunt Linda and Uncle Joe

Kelly's Cannoli Dip

Because I am very picky about my cannoli filling, I usually make my own. I don't like it too sweet. I like mascarpone (a lot!). I also like the ricotta taste too. Sadly, I rarely find cannoli that I like.

Shells are such a hassle - they are time consuming to make and I can't always get to the Italian market to buy empty shells. This dip solves the problem perfectly. Simply use pizzelle cookies, graham crackers, biscotti, or puff pastry dough shells. This way we can have cannoli anytime!! Yummy!

- 3 cups ricotta cheese (drained) it needs to be quite dry
- ½ - ¾ cup mascarpone cheese
- ½ cup (ish) confectioners' (10x) sugar
- 1 teaspoon vanilla
- mini-chocolate chips

Combine first 4 ingredients very well with an electric mixer. Stir in the chocolate chips. Taste and feel free to add a little more sugar if needed.

Fill a bowl with the dip and serve with Pizzelle cookies, graham crackers, biscotti, or whatever suits your fancy!

Mom's Pizzelle Cookies

- 1 ¾ flour
- 2 teaspoons baking powder
- 3 large eggs
- ¾ cup sugar
- ½ cup unsalted butter -melted
- 1or 2 tablespoons anise or vanilla extract (to taste)

Melt butter, cool then add extract. Set aside
Mix flour & baking powder, set aside
Put sugar and eggs in mixer bowl then whip until thick, approximately a minute.
Slowly add butter mix..
Turn mixer to low.
Slowly add flour mixture stop as soon as its combined.. 10 seconds or so. Use a wooden spoon to make sure its mixed. Do not over mix.
Cook on pizzelle maker according to your makers directions.

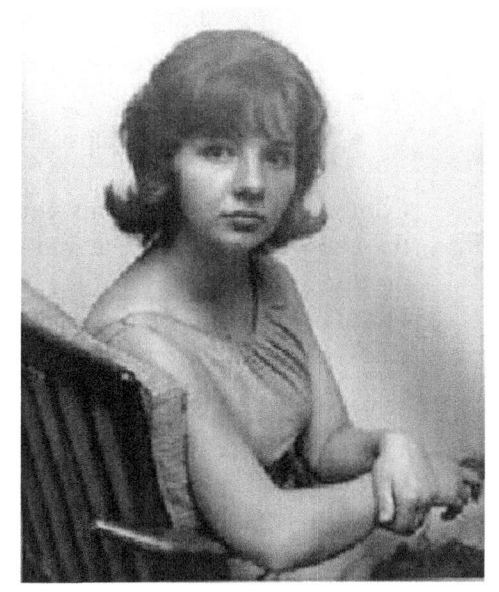

My Mother

Almond Biscotti

Biscotti is best if made a day ahead. Perfect with your morning tea or coffee.

- 1 cup sugar
- 1 stick unsalted butter, melted
- 3 tablespoons brandy
- 2 teaspoons pure almond extract
- 1 teaspoon pure vanilla extract
- 1 cup whole almonds, lightly toasted, cooled, and coarsely chopped
- 3 large eggs
- 2 ¾ cups all-purpose flour
- 1 ½ teaspoons baking powder
- 1 tablespoon fresh orange zest
- ¼ teaspoon salt

Preheat oven to 350°F

In a large bowl, beat the butter and sugar together on medium speed until light and fluffy. Beat in the eggs, one at a time, then the brandy, vanilla and almond extracts until combined, scraping down the bowl and beaters as needed. Stir in almonds and zest. In another bowl stir flour, baking powder, and salt until just combined. Combine wet and dry ingredients. Chill dough, covered, 30 minutes.

Using moist hands, halve dough and form 2 long narrow(2 inch wide) loaves on parchment paper on a baking sheet.

Bake about 30 minutes until pale golden. Carefully transfer loaves to a rack and cool 15 minutes. Lower the oven to 325°.

Carefully slice loaves into ¾-inch slices on the diagonal with a serrated knife. Arrange slice, with a cut side down, on a fresh parchment paper on a baking sheet and bake until golden, 15-25 minutes, flipping carefully halfway through. Transfer to rack to cool completely.

☘ Shortbread cookies

My favorite, enough said.

- 2 sticks of butter softened
- ½ cup of sugar
- 2 cups flour
- $1/8$ teaspoon salt

Preheat oven to 325°

In a large bowl beat butter and sugar together until fluffy. Add flour and salt. With your hands (easiest) or a wooden spoon, rub the flour and creamed butter together gently until you can press the dough together and form a ball The reason your hands are easier is because the warmth of your hands helps the butter and flour blend together faster. Place dough on a lightly flour surface and roll out to about ½ inch think. Cut into traditional rectangle shapes (or any shape and size you desire. We even do cookie cutter shapes - the 'finger' shapes were just easier for those who had them at 'tea-time' they were dainty and easy to dip into your coffee or tea)

Place on ungreased cookie sheet and prick with a fork. *Place cookie sheet in the PRE HEATED oven and immediately turn the oven **DOWN** to 275°. Bake 25 – 30 minutes.* As I said watch the color, you want them still sandy white on top, golden around the edges.

NOTE: To be fancy I sometimes drizzle these with melted chocolate (dark, milk or white) They are yummy that way! On St Patty's day I serve these tradition Celtic cookies with white chocolate that I made green with food coloring.

☘ MaryJo's Molasses Cookies

- ¾ cup butter
- 1 cup packed brown sugar
- ¼ cup cold strong coffee
- ¼ cup dark molasses
- 1 egg
- 2 cups flour
- ¼ teaspoon salt
- 2 teaspoons baking soda
- 1 teaspoon cinnamon
- 1 teaspoon cloves
- 1 teaspoon ginger

My Mother in law, MaryJo

Preheat oven to 375°
Using your mixer, beat butter until fluffy. Then beat in the sugar. Next add the egg, coffee, and molasses. Combine all very well. Then add the rest of the ingredients. Mix together very well. Put the soft dough in the refrigerator for a few hours. This step is very important. I made them without chilling and they do not come out as well.
On parchment covered cookie sheets, drop by rounded teaspoonful - these do spread so space the dough.
Bake about 9 minutes...very very important these should look just short of done. They should look like they should bake another 1-2 minutes but DON'T do it. These cookies will 'deflate' as they cool. These are a soft chewy cookie.

🍀 Aunt Claire's Irish Cream

Alert: This recipe contains raw eggs. If you are serving this beverage to the elderly, immune compromised, or children use pasteurized egg that you can find in the refrigerated section of the grocery store.

- 10 oz Rye Whisky (or Irish Whiskey)
- 1 (14 oz) can of sweetened condensed milk
- 1 cup half and half
- 1 teaspoon coconut extract
- 2 eggs
- 2 tablespoons chocolate syrup

Blend all ingredients in a blender until well mixed.
Chill well.
Shake well before serving.

My Grandparents, Dad, and Aunt Barbara

Affogato al caffe

- 3 – 4 ounces espresso (or double brewed strong coffee)
- 1 scoop vanilla ice cream or gelato

For each Affogato you wish to make. Place one scoop of ice cream into each mug or dessert dish.

Pour about 3 or 4 ounces of hot espresso over the ice cream. Sprinkle with chopped toasted almonds or a dash of cinnamon if desired.

Limoncello

This recipe takes time but is worth the wait.
You will need to sterilize the containers you steep the mixture in as well as the bottles you plan to store your limoncello in.

- 1 liter grain alcohol such as EverClear / or use 90- 100 proof vodka
- 10 lemons
- 5 cups water
- 4 cups granulated sugar

Wash well and dry your lemons, since you're going to be using the peel exclusively. Next, using a vegetable peeler, peel your lemons - you don't want the white pith under the peel, so try to peel as thinly as possible. Put the peels into a large glass container that has a lid.

Add the alcohol, making sure that it completely covers the peels. Next, let the mixture sit undisturbed for 1- 2 weeks.

Place a colander inside a large bowl. Shake mixture well. Pour the alcohol mixture into the colander and drain, using a wooden spoon to press out any excess liquid from the peels. Discard the peels.

Stir the water and sugar in a large saucepan over medium heat until the sugar dissolves, about 5 minutes. Cool completely. Pour the sugar syrup over the vodka mixture. Cover and let stand at room temperature overnight. Then stir well with a wooden spoon.

Place a wire mesh strainer over a large, clean bowl and place a coffee filter inside the mesh strainer. Slowly pour the limoncello through the coffee filter. replacing the coffee filter with a new one as needed and continue until all of the limoncello has been filtered.

Next, filter again and fill individual bottles. Place a funnel into the mouth of the bottle you'll use for your finished limoncello. Place a coffee filter inside the funnel, and slowly pour the limoncello through the coffee filter to fill the bottle. Seal the bottle(s) and store in the fridge up to a month or in the freezer indefinitely.

Index

Chapter 1 : The Basics 7

  Roasting Garlic 8

  Clarified Butter (ghee) 9

  Roasted Red Pepper 10

  Basic Chicken Stock 11

  Basic White Sauce (Béchamel) 13

  Basic Pizza Dough 14

  Basic Tomato Sauce 15

  Basic Pasta Dough 16

  Caramelized Onions 17

  Italian Vinaigrette 17

  Basic Pesto 18

  Basic Risotto 19

Chapter 2 : Soups & Starters 21

  Kelly's Cock-a Leekie Soup 22

  Potato Leek Soup 23

  White Onion Soup 24

  Brotchan Roy 25

  Pastina with Egg Broth 26

  My Mama's Pastina al latte 27

  Tomato Bread Soup 28

  My Favorite Minestrone 29

  Aunt Theresa's Pasta E Fagioli (Pasta and Beans) 30

  Easy Escarole Soup 31

  Aunt Louise's Clams Oreganato 31

  Aunt Louise's Clams Oreganato 32

  Bruschetta 33

  Mom's Stuffed Artichoke 34

  Pratie Oaten (Potato Cakes) 35

Chapter 3 : Breads 36

  Nana's Irish Soda Bread 37

  Tea Bannocks 38

  Irish Buttermilk Bread 39

  Rosemary and Sea Salt Flatbread 40

  Tuscan Bread 41

  Italian Bread Bowls 42

  Mom's Italian Easter Egg Bread 43

  Rustic Italian Bread 45

Chapter 4 : Sides 46

  Honeyed Parsnips 47

  Baked Leeks and Cream 48

  Colcannon and Champ 48

  Colcannon 49

  Champ 49

  Creamy Polenta with Cheese 50

  Fried Potatoes and Peppers 51

Insalata Caprese 52

Chapter 5 : Entree 53

Saltimbocca 54

Dublin Coddle 55

Mom's Braciole 56

Fish Cakes 57

Irish Fry 58

MaryJo's Boiled Dinner 59

Slow Cooker Italian Sandwiches 60

Beef Stew in Stout 61

Linguini and White Clam Sauce 62

Kelly's Italian Style Macaroni and Cheese 62

Kelly's Italian Style Macaroni and Cheese 63

Aunt Mary's

Semolina Pasta 64

Aunt Linda's Sunday Gravy 65

Aunt Linda's Meatballs 66

Vodka Sauce 67

Nana's Kidney Stew over Noodles 68

Chapter 6 : Desserts and Treats 70

Grandma's Italian Bowtie Cookies 71

Nevatels 72

Nevatels 73

Chocolate Syrup 74

Grandma's Struffoli 74

Grandma's Struffoli 75

Nana's Baked Rice Pudding 76

Bread and Butter

Pudding 77

Kelly's Cannoli Dip 78

Kelly's Cannoli Dip 79

Mom's Pizzelle Cookies 80

Almond Biscotti 80

Almond Biscotti 81

Shortbread cookies 82

MaryJo's Molasses Cookies 83

Aunt Claire's Irish Cream 84

Affogato al caffe 85

Limoncello 86

Index 87

About the Author 89

About the Author

Kelly Schweiger, although born in New York City, grew up in the country and married a farmer. She lives in an old farm house in upstate NY with her husband Fred and her four children, Sarah, Matthew, Jacob, and Noah. With a knack for making 'something out of nothing' and a passion for trying new foods and flavors, she puts a fresh new spin on old fashioned recipes and traditional cooking. Kelly cooks with real ingredients and is definitely not afraid of butter! Kelly writes a food blog, A Chaotic Cook, and enjoys spending time with her family, reading, writing, computers, acting in her local community theater and of course cooking and baking. She can generally be found in her tiny, chaotic, galley kitchen cooking for her family…and anyone else who happens to stop by or look hungry.

Made in the USA
Middletown, DE
19 November 2023

43072814R00056